We Can Do It Together

Working as a Team

Leonard Clasky

SOCiAL AND EMOTiONAL LEARNiNG
FOR THE REAL WORLD™

Rosen Classroom™

Teamwork is an important tool.
You can use it at home
and at school.

You can't score a goal alone.
You need your team to help!

Your friend can pass you
the soccer ball.
Then you can score the goal!

You can't finish a big science
project alone.
You need your team to help!

Your classmates can help you.
You can write notes.
They can present to the class.

You can't clean the whole house alone.
You need your family to help!

A grown-up can clean the floors.
You can do the dishes.

Working as a team means
being fair.
Treat everyone with respect.

Working as a team means
talking it out.
Listen to what others have to say.

If you work as a team,
then you can get it done!

Words to Know

dishes

project

soccer ball